# Write On...
# DINOSAURS

## CONTENTS

# Age of the dinosaurs

Dinosaurs were reptiles that lived on Earth millions of years ago. The first ones appeared more than 240 million years ago (mya), and the last ones died out around 65 mya.

We know about dinosaurs from fossils – rocks that have preserved ancient bones, teeth or even footprints. People who study fossils are called palaeontologists (say *pal-ee-on-tol-a-jists*). So far, they have found more than 300 types of dinosaur – but there are probably up to 900 types left to be discovered!

## The Mesozoic era

Palaeontologists call the age of the dinosaurs the Mesozoic era, meaning the 'middle life era' – it's the second of three eras since life first appeared.

The world looked very different millions of years ago. When dinosaurs first appeared, all the land was joined up – the continents hadn't pulled apart yet.

The Mesozoic era is split into three smaller stretches of time: the Triassic, Jurassic and Cretaceous periods. Each of those still lasted millions of years!

Pangaea is the name of the super-continent that existed at the start of the Mesozoic era.

4

# Write On...

Think about the climate when you set the scene for a story. The Triassic period was hot and dry. How do you think that affected the behaviour of Triassic animals?

This illustration shows dinosaurs that were around during the Cretaceous.

# Record breakers

We already know about hundreds of species of dinosaur – and fossils of new ones are being found all the time! These ancient reptiles included meat- and plant-eaters and they came in many shapes and sizes …

 The earliest known dinosaur was Nyasaurus. It lived in what is now East Africa 243 mya.

 The first dinosaur to be named was Megalosaurus in 1824. Its name means 'great lizard'.

 The largest dinosaur was a cousin of Argentinosaurus that doesn't have a name yet. It weighed as much as fourteen African elephants.

 Relative to its size, Troodon was the brainiest dinosaur. Even so, it was not much cleverer than a chicken!

  The heaviest theropod (meat-eating dinosaur) was 20-tonne Spinosaurus.

Spinosaurus is the largest known theropod. It lived around 100 mya.

# Write On...

Superlatives are adjectives that are perfect for describing record-breakers. Examples include **best**, **greatest**, **supreme**, **formidable**, **unrivalled** and **unbeatable**.

# Mighty meat-eaters

Tyrannosaurus rex has to be the most famous dinosaur of all. This terrifying hunter had huge, powerful jaws. When chasing its prey it could cover 8 m in a single second!

T. rex belonged to a group of dinosaurs we call theropods, which ate meat and walked or ran on two legs. Some theropods were small and speedy but the scariest were huge like T. rex. They had massive skulls on short necks, long tails and small arms.

## Big bruisers

T. rex lived in what's now North America right at the end of the Cretaceous. Other mighty meat-eaters from that time were Carnotaurus in South America and T. rex's close relative Tarbosaurus in China. The big hunter Allosaurus lived about ninety million years earlier, in the Jurassic.

Carnotaurus was a large theropod with a short, deep skull. It had horns like a bull's, one above each eye.

# Write On...

Write your own multiple-choice dinosaur quiz. Think of ways to trick people into choosing a wrong answer or make them laugh! For example, the answer options for **What was T. rex's Asian cousin called?** could be: **a) Tarbosaurus; b) Turbosaurus;** or **c) Soysaucesus.**

T. rex had more than sixty teeth. They were up to 23 cm long.

9

# Pack hunters

The biggest theropods hunted solo because they were powerful enough to take down large prey on their own. Smaller predators were successful by teaming up in groups or packs, just like wolves and hunting dogs today.

Dromaeosaurus was the first pack hunter to be named by palaeontologists. It was a small, feathered theropod that lived in North America in the Cretaceous. Dromaeosaurus had a big, curved claw on each foot for gripping prey and extremely sharp teeth for tearing into its meaty meals.

## The dromaeosaurs

Over the last century, palaeontologists have found other dinosaurs with the same features, such as Velociraptor and Deinonychus. They call them the dromaeosaurs. Utahraptor is the largest known dromaeosaur. It was about the size of a polar bear.

Dromaeosaurus probably reached speeds of 60 kph. Its name means 'running lizard'.

A Velociraptor pack attacks a larger meat-eater, Tarbosaurus.

# Write On...

Alliteration – when words start with the same sound – adds rhythm to your writing. Examples include **curved claw**, **teeth for tearing** or **meaty meals**. Try some of your own.

Utahraptor's killer claw was probably up to 24 cm long. Ouch!

# Bird-like beasts

For decades, dinosaur experts thought dinosaurs were all scaly-skinned like today's reptiles. Then, about twenty years ago, they found the first fossil of a feathered dinosaur.

Sinosauropteryx was discovered in China in 1995. Since then, experts have identified dozens more theropods that had feathers. The first feathers were probably frayed scales that had gone fluffy. Therizinosaurus was covered in fluff, which probably kept it warm.

Therizinosaurus was one of the biggest feathered dinosaurs. It had outsize, bladelike claws or 'scissorhands'.

### From fluff to feathers

Later, fluff turned into feathers for showing off. Long feathers on the arms, or 'wings', gave dinosaurs a bit of lift if they were running, leaping or gliding. At some point, these winged, feathered dinosaurs evolved into birds (see pages 26–27).

Archaeopteryx lived 150 mya and was known as the oldest bird. However, recent fossils of early birds found in China date back to 160 mya.

# Write On...

No one knows if dinosaur feathers were as colourful as some modern birds' – so your imagination can run riot! Use a thesaurus to find alternative colour names, such as **scarlet** or **ruby** instead of **red.**

Gigantoraptor was a whopping 8 m long! The feathers on its wings helped him to run super-fast.

# Boneheads

Hadrosaurs were common in the Cretaceous period. They lived together in groups. They had bulky bodies and hard, bony skulls that could be flat, bumpy or spectacularly crested.

Hadrosaurs such as Pachycephalosaurus and Stegoceras had big, bony domes on their skulls. Rival males may have fought each other by headbutting, just like stags today. The skulls would have acted like crash helmets to protect their brains.

## Attracting attention

Hadrosaurs' crests were probably brightly coloured, for showing off. Some crests were hollow. Experts think these were a way of attracting attention, too. The crests worked like loudspeakers, turning the hadrosaurs' calls into loud, booming noises!

Hadrosaurs are sometimes called the duckbills, because of their long, flat snouts and beak-shaped mouths.

Although hadrosaurs had toothless 'beaks', their cheeks were packed with tiny teeth for grinding up vegetation – some had nearly a thousand!

Parasaurolophus had a 1.8-m-long crest. It may have made low, deep noises like a foghorn!

# Write On...

If you're struggling to start a story, try a sound effect such as **BA-DA-BOOM!** It's a good way to attract attention – and then you can explain the **where**, **what** and **why** of the noise.

# Armoured dinosaurs

These big plant-eaters grazed in herds for safety, but that wasn't enough to scare off hungry meat-eaters. They also had additional defences, including horns, spikes, clubs and thick skin that acted as armour.

 Ceratopsians were dinosaurs with a horns and a big neck frill. Triceratops and Torosaurus were both ceratopsians.

 Torosaurus had one of the biggest skulls of any land animal ever! With its neck frill, it was about 2.8 m — as long as a family car!

 Ankylosaurus had bony lumps and spikes on its back and a heavy club at the end of its tail. Perhaps the club had eye-like markings to confuse meat-eaters!

 Stegosaurus had four spikes at the end of its tail, each up to 90 cm long. It could whip its tail round to slash at an attacker.

 Stegosaurus and its relatives had diamond-shaped plates along their backs, perhaps for keeping their body temperature steady.

Triceratops uses its three sharp horns to defend itself against predators.

# Write On...

Describing words help to build up a sense of character – even for dinosaurs! For the armoured dinosaurs, try adjectives such as **shambling**, **bumbling** and **bulky**.

# Lumbering giants

The biggest dinosaurs were gentle giants, not ferocious meat-eaters. Sauropods were dinosaurs with long necks and enormous bodies. They lumbered along on all fours looking for plants to eat.

Everything about sauropods was giant … except for their heads and brains! Even the largest sauropods had brains no bigger than tennis balls. They didn't need much intelligence, though. Living in herds and being enormous helped to protect them from predators. All they had to do was eat, eat, eat!

## Eating machines

Being so huge meant that sauropods needed to eat a lot of vegetation – perhaps as much as half a tonne a day. They probably fed by sweeping their necks from side to side to snatch up food, then swallowing it down without chewing.

Early palaeontologists thought sauropods were too huge to support their own weight on land. They thought they must have lived in water like whales.

Sauropods' necks were up to 15 m long – that's six times longer than a giraffe's!

This Tapuiasaurus herd is on the move.

# Write On...

Instead of using the verb **go**, find alternatives that will be more descriptive. Try **lumber** for slow-movers and **dart** for speedy ones.

# Babies and eggs

Like today's reptiles, mother dinosaurs laid eggs in shallow nests in the ground. Plant-eaters produced round eggs, some bigger than footballs! Meat-eaters laid oval eggs – the smallest known were just 11 cm.

An amazing Saltasaurus nesting site was discovered in 1997. There were hundreds of eggs and even some sauropod embryos (developing babies).

The first dinosaur egg fossils were found in Mongolia in the 1920s. They belonged to Oviraptor. It got its name, which means 'egg thief', because experts thought for a long time that the eggs belonged to another dinosaur, Protoceratops.

## Perfect parents

The first evidence that dinosaurs cared for their young came from hadrosaur nesting sites in Montana, USA. Fossils of weak youngsters showed that parents must have brought food to their offspring. The hadrosaur was named Maiasaura, meaning 'good mother lizard'.

Baby dinosaurs grew amazingly fast. Maiasaura hatchlings were just 30 cm long; by the age of one, they were ten times as long!

## Write On...

Write an account of discovering a dinosaur egg fossil. Is it easier to capture the excitement if you write in the first person (**I**) or the third person (**he** or **she**)?

An Oviraptor feeds
a dead lizard to
its hungry young.

21

# Sea reptiles

Dinosaurs ruled the land in the Mesozoic era, but not the ocean. There, many kinds of ancient marine reptiles fed on plants, fish, other sea creatures ... and each other!

Ichthyosaurs were dolphin-shaped hunters that could move smoothly through the water. Some were just a metre long. Others were more than 20 m. Many had huge eyes. These helped to let in as much light as possible when ichthyosaurs were hunting squid in the ocean depths. One species had eyes as big as dinner plates!

## Big paddlers

Plesiosaurs were the sauropods of the seas because they had enormously long necks! Instead of legs, though, they had flippers for swimming. Elasmosaurus was one of the largest at 14 m long. Pliosaurs were close cousins of plesiosaurs. They had flippers, too, but their necks were short.

Liopleurodon was a large pliosaur that lived around 155 mya. It hunted ichthyosaurs.

All marine reptiles had to come up to the surface to breathe air.

In 1810, Joseph and Mary Anning found an Ichthyosaurus fossil in Lyme Regis, England. It was the first discovery of an ancient reptile's whole skeleton.

# Write On...

The trick to building up tension is to go slow. Don't let a predator catch its prey instantly. Describe it **lurking** and **closing in**. An ellipsis (...) can help to create a sense of suspense.

# Flying reptiles

Flying reptiles ruled the skies during the Mesozoic era – these were the pterosaurs, or 'winged lizards'. The smallest were robin-sized, but the biggest were the largest flying creatures ever!

 Pterosaurs' beaks came in many shapes. Pterodaustro had a jaw packed with bristles for sieving out sea creatures. Dimorphodon's beak was like a puffin's.

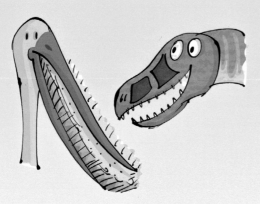

 Pterosaurs did not have feathers. Their wings were leathery and their skin was scaly. Some had downy hair on their bodies for warmth.

 Some pterosaurs, such as Rhamphorhynchus, had a long tail to help them steer. It had a flap at the end like a rudder.

 Pterodactylus was probably the earliest pterosaur fossil that people found. It was put on display in the 1770s.

 Tropeognathus had a record-breaking 8-m wingspan – almost as wide as a hang glider's!

This fish-eater, Anhanguera, had a 4.5-m wingspan.

# Write On...

Think about verbs to do with flying, such as **swoop**, **soar** and **plummet**. If you use them to describe moods instead of actual flight, the words become metaphors — they're comparing feelings to flying.

# End of the dinosaurs

Dinosaurs were on Earth for more than 175 million years – that's nearly 900 times longer than we modern humans have existed! Then, 65 mya, they became extinct (died out).

No one is certain why the dinosaurs died out. The most popular idea is that a huge piece of space rock – a meteorite, asteroid or comet – crashed into Earth. The impact would have killed everything in the immediate area and thrown up enough dust to block out the Sun for decades. Without sunlight, plants would have died, then plant-eaters and then meat-eaters.

## Survivors

Not all animals became extinct at the end of the Mesozoic. On land, smaller mammals, reptiles and amphibians survived, as well as insects and spiders. Now the dinosaurs had gone, they could rule the Earth instead!

Dinosaurs became extinct 65 mya, but their relatives still live on Earth! Today's birds are all theropods, from the same group of animals as fearsome T. rex!

A giant meteorite hitting the Earth might explain why many species went extinct at the end of the Mesozoic.

Not only dinosaurs died out 65 mya. Around three-quarters of plants and animals were wiped out, including pterosaurs and marine reptiles.

# Write On...

If you're writing a factual report about an event, it's a good idea to keep these questions in mind: **what?**, **where?**, **who?**, **why?**, **when?** and **how?**

# Write On... Writing school

Are you ready to show off some of the terrific dinosaur facts you've found out? First, decide on your form. Here are some ideas:

 A set of Top Trumps®–style cards about different dinosaurs and other prehistoric reptiles. Research their statistics and add a short description of each one, too.

 A poem describing a peaceful Jurassic scene, suddenly destroyed by the appearance of a hungry Allosaurus.

 An advert or poster for a dinosaur safari park, where there are life-like robotic dinosaurs on the loose.

 If you like drawing, you can always tell a story through a comic strip, like the one below about an amazing fossil find.

PALAEONTOLOGISTS WERE ON A DIG IN THE GOBI DESERT. THE YEAR WAS 1994. ONE SPOTTED BONES AND CLAWS - IT WAS A FOSSIL!

AFTER CLEANING UP THE FIND, THE TEAM SAW THAT THE FOSSIL SHOWED AN OVIRAPTOR SITTING ON ITS NEST OF EGGS.

HAD OVIRAPTOR BEEN KILLED WHILE PROTECTING HER EGGS FROM AN APPROACHING SANDSTORM? IT LOOKED LIKE HER 'WINGS' WERE SHIELDING THE NEST!

Try your hand at a bit of science-fiction. Write a short story in which scientists are bringing dinosaurs back to life from prehistoric samples of DNA. Your opening could be like this:

"Finally!" Emma announced. "The result of years of work ... I am very proud to introduce you to little Deino!"

There was a gasp as the scientist drew back the curtain. Her life's ambition had been to rebuild a dinosaur from preserved DNA and she'd finally done it.

The caged Deinonychus made an ominous growl ...

Look online for photos to illustrate your story.

# Glossary

**crest** A body part that sticks up from an animal's head, and is usually ornamental.

**Cretaceous period** The time from 145 to 65 million years ago, and the third period that makes up the Mesozoic era.

**DNA** The special instructions that give every living thing its characteristics.

**evolve** How one species changes into another species, over millions of years, by passing on particular characteristics to the next generation.

**extinct** Describes an animal or plant that has disappeared from the world forever.

**flipper** A flat 'leg' that has evolved to help an animal move through water.

**fossil** The remains of an animal or plant that died long ago, preserved in rock.

**frill** A bony area around a dinosaur's neck.

**Jurassic period** The time from 206 to 145 million years ago, and the second period that makes up the Mesozoic era.

**marine** Living in the sea.

**Mesozoic era** The time from 251 to 65 million years ago.

**palaeontologist** A scientist who studies fossils.

**plate** A protective, bony section on a reptile's skin.

**plesiosaur** A long-necked, predatory marine reptile of the Jurassic and Cretaceous.

**predator** An animal that hunts and eats other animals for food.

**prehistoric** Before the time of written history.

**prey** An animal that is hunted and eaten by other animals for food.

**pterosaur** A flying reptile with wings made from skin stretched over a long fourth finger.

**sauropod** A huge, long-necked, plant-eating saurischian (lizard-hipped) dinosaur that walked on all fours.

**species** One particular type of living thing. Members of the same species look similar and can produce offspring together.

**theropod** A two-legged, meat-eating saurischian (lizard-hipped) dinosaur with sharp teeth and claws.

**Triassic period** The time from 251 to 206 million years ago, and the first period that makes up the Mesozoic era.

**vegetation** Plants.

# Further reading and websites

**READ MORE ABOUT DINOSAURS:**
**Dinosaur Survival Guide** by Clare Hibbert (Arcturus Publishing, 2016)

**Know it All: Dinosaurs** by Andrew Langley (Franklin Watts, 2015)

**Knowledge Encyclopedia: Dinosaur!** (Dorling Kindersley, 2014)

**READ MORE ABOUT BEING A GREAT WRITER:**
**How to Write a Story** by Simon Cheshire (Bloomsbury, 2014)

**How to Write Your Best Story Ever!** by Christopher Edge
(Oxford University Press, 2015)

**The Usborne Write Your Own Story Book** (Usborne Publishing, 2011)

**DISCOVER MORE ABOUT DINOSAURS ONLINE:**
**www.bbc.co.uk/nature/prehistoric**
View some of the best series about prehistoric life ever broadcast
by the BBC.

**www.luisrey.ndtilda.co.uk**
Visit a gallery of artwork by one of the world's foremost dinosaur artists.

**http://www.nhm.ac.uk/discover/dino-directory/index.html**
The Natural History Museum in London, UK's online guide to dinosaurs.

# Index

Look for the pronunciation guide (how to say the word) in small type after the name of each dinosaur or other prehistoric creature.